T0066205

4   ANGIE

11   COLD AS ICE

16   COME SAIL AWAY

28   DON'T FEAR THE REAPER

32   GREEN-EYED LADY

21   HEY JUDE

38   IF YOU LEAVE ME NOW

43   NIGHTS IN WHITE SATIN

48   PROUD MARY

56   REELING IN THE YEARS

60   ROSANNA

51   SCHOOL'S OUT

64   SHE'S ALWAYS A WOMAN

71   TINY DANCER

78   WALK THIS WAY

74   WE ARE THE CHAMPIONS

ANGIE

Words and Music by MICK JAGGER
and KEITH RICHARDS

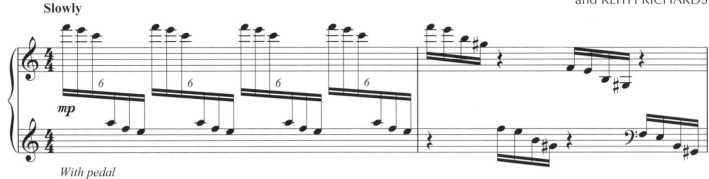

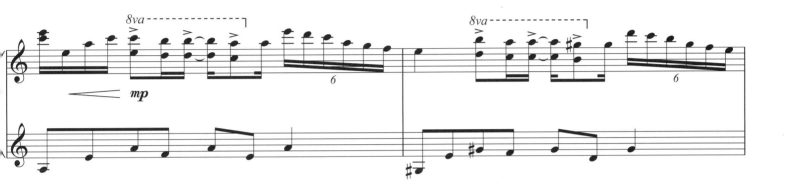

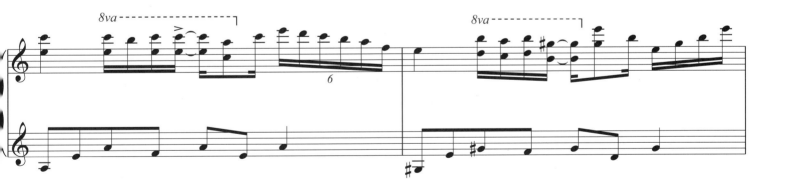

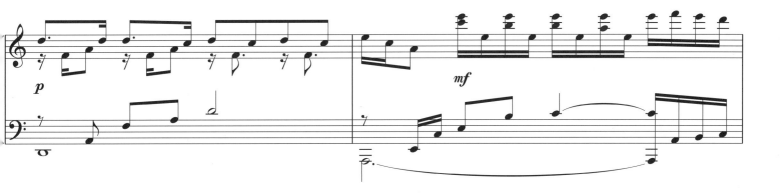

COLD AS ICE

Words and Music by MICK JONES
and LOU GRAMM

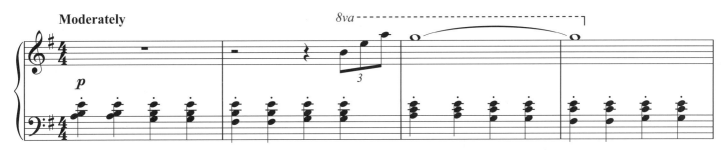

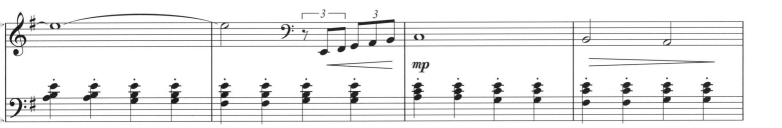

COME SAIL AWAY

Words and Music by
DENNIS DeYOUNG

Slow and stately

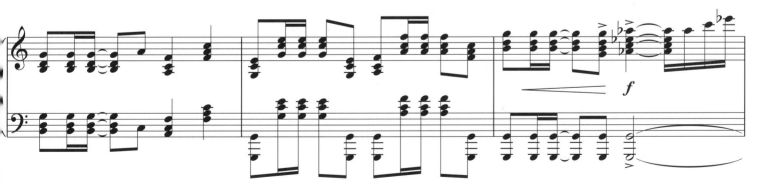

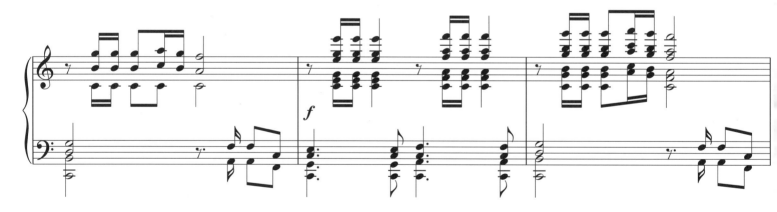

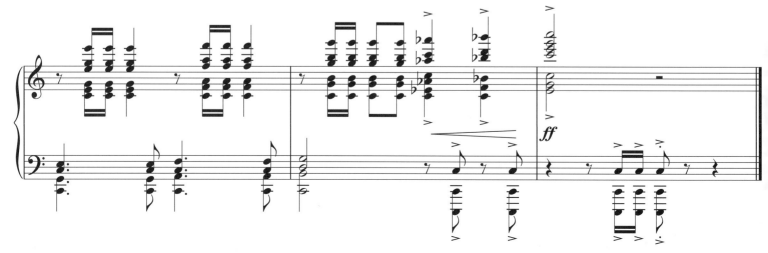

HEY JUDE

Words and Music by JOHN LENNON
and PAUL McCARTNEY

Slowly and steadily

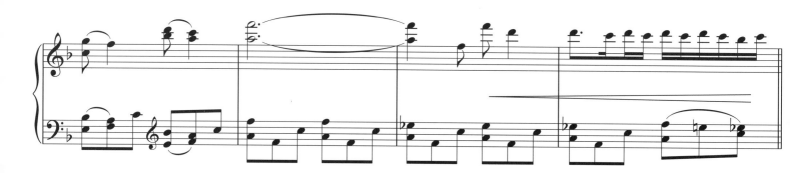

DON'T FEAR THE REAPER

Words and Music by
DONALD ROESER

To Coda ⊕

with pedal

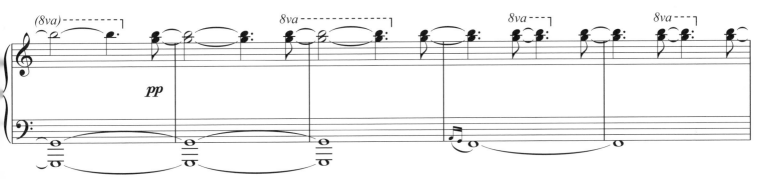

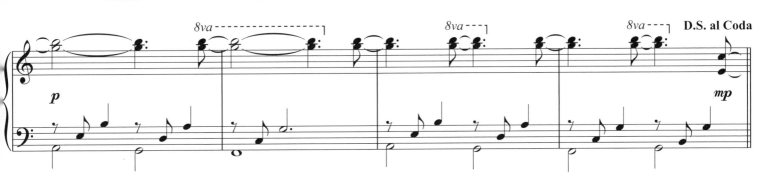

GREEN-EYED LADY

Words and Music by JERRY CORBETTA,
J.C. PHILLIPS and DAVID RIORDAN

Moderately fast, with a driving beat

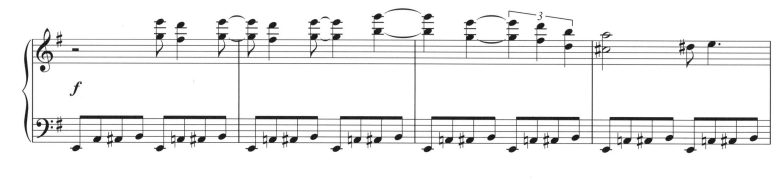

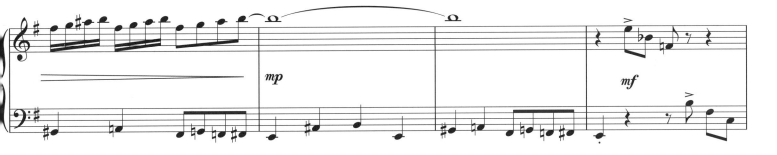

36

IF YOU LEAVE ME NOW

Words and Music by
PETER CETERA

Moderately

mp *poco stacatto*

NIGHTS IN WHITE SATIN

Words and Music by
JUSTIN HAYWARD

Slowly, gently rocking

PROUD MARY

Words and Music by
JOHN FOGERTY

Smoothly rolling

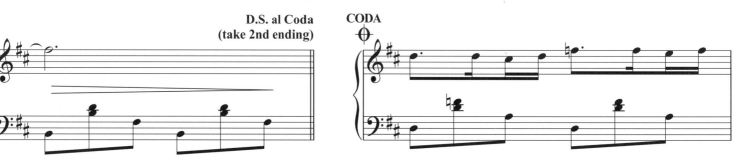

SCHOOL'S OUT

Words and Music by MICHAEL BRUCE,
GLEN BUXTON, ALICE COOPER,
DENNIS DUNAWAY and NEAL SMITH

Moderately fast, pulsing

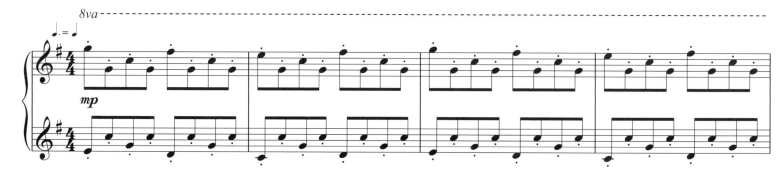

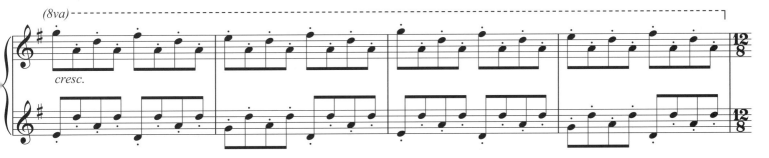

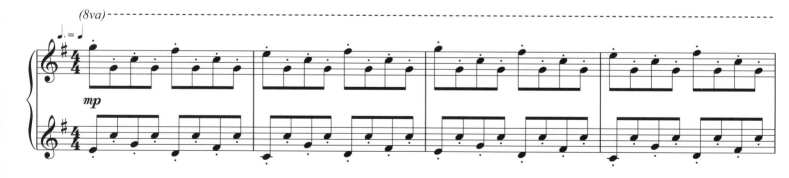

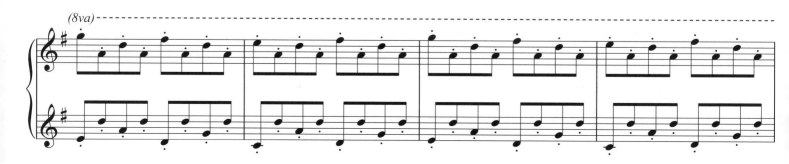

REELING IN THE YEARS

Words and Music by WALTER BECKER
and DONALD FAGEN

ROSANNA

Words and Music by
DAVID PAICH

Fast, energetic

SHE'S ALWAYS A WOMAN

Words and Music by
BILLY JOEL

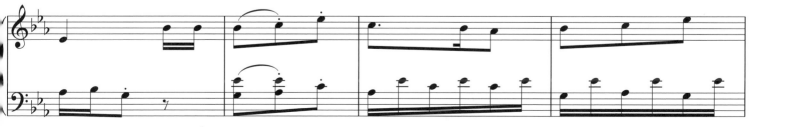

To Coda ⊕

D.S. al Coda

70

CODA

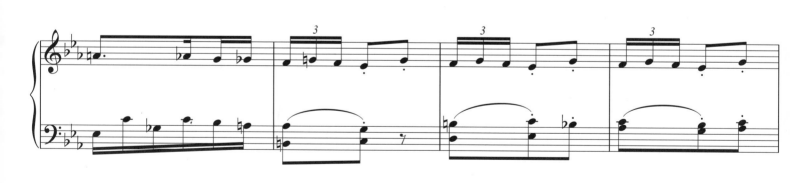

TINY DANCER

Words and Music by ELTON JOHN
and BERNIE TAUPIN

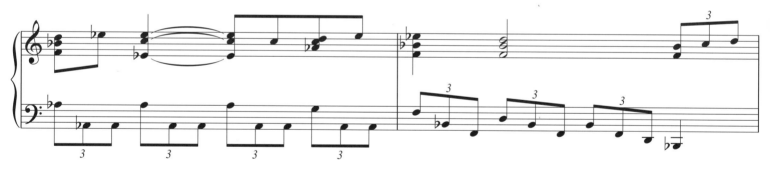

D.S. al Coda

CODA

WE ARE THE CHAMPIONS

Words and Music by
FREDDIE MERCURY

Animated and driving

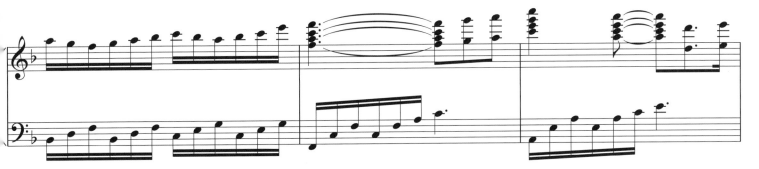

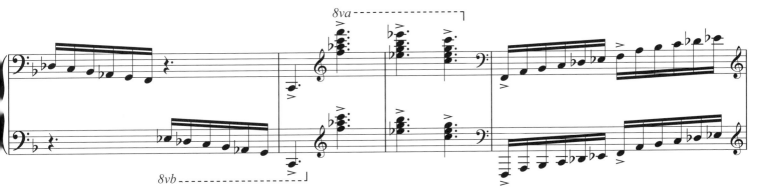

WALK THIS WAY

Words and Music by STEVEN TYLER
and JOE PERRY

Disney
Favorites
FOR ACCORDION

ISBN 978-1-5400-9423-0

Disney Characters and Artwork © Disney
Disney/Pixar elements © Disney/Pixar

The following songs are the property of:

Bourne Co.
Music Publishers
www.bournemusic.com

BABY MINE
SOME DAY MY PRINCE WILL COME
WHEN YOU WISH UPON A STAR
WHISTLE WHILE YOU WORK

Visit Hal Leonard Online at
www.halleonard.com

Contact us:
Hal Leonard
7777 West Bluemound Road
Milwaukee, WI 53213
Email: info@halleonard.com

In Europe, contact:
Hal Leonard Europe Limited
42 Wigmore Street
Marylebone, London, W1U 2RN
Email: info@halleonardeurope.com

In Australia, contact:
Hal Leonard Australia Pty. Ltd.
4 Lentara Court
Cheltenham, Victoria, 3192 Australia
Email: info@halleonard.com.au

CONTENTS

3   Baby Mine

6   Evermore

12   For the First Time in Forever

19   Hakuna Matata

24   He's a Pirate

29   Into the Unknown

36   Remember Me (Ernesto de la Cruz)

40   Some Day My Prince Will Come

48   Speechless

43   That's How You Know

62   When You Wish Upon a Star

54   Whistle While You Work

58   You've Got a Friend in Me